British Battlefields Series

Preston 1648

Dr. Richard Holmes

Contents

Illustrations

Oliver Cromwell
The Duke of Hamilton
The Earl of Collander
Major-General Lambert
Sir Marmaduke Langdale
A Pikeman

A Musketeer
The Lower Hodder Bridge
Watery Lane
The Eaves Brook from Ribbleton Lane
Preston from the south, 1728
The Battle of Preston by Charles Cattermole

Maps

The Preston Campaign

Preston and its surroundings

Writing the history of any battle is never easy. Participants, caught up in a traumatic crisis, recall events in a patchy, sporadic fashion. If they subsequently commit their recollections to paper, they may—while striving to tell the truth as they saw it—produce an account which is at best subjective and at worst decidedly partisan. Writing the history of a Seventeenth-Century battle is especially difficult. Of the small number of eyewitnesses who chose to record their experiences, few had access to watch, and fewer still to an accurate map. It follows, therefore, that the historian of a Civil War battle must, of necessity, pick his way with care, treading softly amongst sources which are usually incomplete and sometimes contradictory.

The battle of Preston presents particular problems. Although the three main Parliamentarian accounts, those of Lieutenant-General Oliver Cromwell, Captain John Hodgson and Captain Samuel Birch, agree in substance, they are somewhat vague as to details of timings and topography. Accounts written by—or on behalf of—the senior officers of the Scots-Royalist force are similarly weak on what modern military historians would regard as essential detail, and have the added difficulty of being written, in whole or in part, with partisan motives, so that they sometimes clash over major issues.

In writing this account of Preston I have attempted, where possible, to rationalise the conflict between sources. I acknowledge, however, that doubt must still surround the precise timings of events on 17 August 1648, as well as the details of communications between the Duke of Hamilton and Sir Marmaduke Langdale on that fateful day.

It is easier to be sure of topography. Although Preston has grown immensely since the battle, the ravages of "town planning" cannot quite conceal the paths of the contending armies. Preston itself was very much smaller in 1648 than it is today. As Dr Richard Kuerden's fine map of 1684 shows, Preston consisted of little more than an agglomeration of houses around the market place, with a few hundred yards of ribbon building along Churchgate, Friargate and Fishergate. In

1675 John Ogilby, in his monumental *Britannia*, described Preston as "six furlongs [1320 yards] in length, large fair and well frequented." He pointed to the town's importance as the major market town in central Lancashire by adding that there were three weekly markets, on Wednesday, Friday, and Saturday.

Walton Bridge—then about 75 yards west of the present structure—was quite distinct from the town, and was connected to it by a main road which followed more or less the line of the present London Road, and by the Stoneygate Lane footpath (perfectly passable to pack-horses) which ran roughly where Manchester Road and Swill Brook Lane now do. The Buck brothers' 1728 engraving of Preston from the south shows quite clearly how Walton bridge and the cottages around it stood separate from the town even eighty years after the battle, and emphasises the importance of the Swill Brook (now culverted for most of its length).

The first phase of the battle proper, the fight between Cromwell and Langdale, took place where Ribbleton Lane crosses the Eaves Brook. This area, much of it enclosed even at the time of the battle, is now heavily built up, although the Eaves Brook still meanders its way along its boggy valley, its flow impeded by litter and discarded supermarket trolleys. Nevertheless, it is clear just how much the present Ribbleton Lane has been raised and easy to imagine how "deep and ill" the lane must have been when it ran straight through the little valley. The area of Ribbleton Moor has also been built on, though patches of open ground between the Eaves Brook and Brockholes Wood, and around the cemetery, give an inkling of what it was once like. Watery Lane still runs down the escarpment towards the Ribble very much as it did three and a half centuries ago: indeed, in the spring of 1985 it was a fair approximation to a Seventeenth-Century lane.

In placing the first phase of the battle where Ribbleton Lane crosses the Eaves Brook I am aware that I dissent from the Ordnance Survey (and thus from David Smurthwaite's otherwise admirable *Battlefields of Britain*) which shows the battle as having taken place in Fulwood. My reasons for doing so are numerous. Firstly, while there is archaeological evidence to support both sites, the discovery of cannon-balls in Fulwood in the last century is unhelpful, for neither Cromwell nor his opponents had cannon at the battle. Secondly, all the evidence suggests that

Cromwell, making his best speed from Longridge to Preston, would have followed the most direct route, which was, then as now, along Ribbleton Lane. Thirdly, it is difficult to imagine how Hamilton, his guard and his rearguard cavalry, who were drawn up on Preston Moor (now Moor Park) could have been so ill-informed of a battle less than a mile away in Fulwood. Fourthly, near-contemporary maps in the County Record Office, showing Ribbleton Lane, the enclosures around it and Ribbleton Moor to the south, tally closely with eyewitness accounts of the battle. Finally, we know that while Cromwell's cavalry pursued the beaten Royalists into the town Ashton's Lancastrians outflanked them to reach Walton Bridge. It is very much easier to envisage this happening with the battle at the Eaves Brook—Ribbleton Lane site than with Ordnance Survey's site in Fulwood.

My research was greatly assisted by the very considerable local knowledge of Mr Alistair C. Hodge, an authority on Seventeenth-Century Lancashire. Without his guidance my task would have been infinitely harder: he has been most generous with his knowledge and his time. Both the Harris Museum and Art Gallery, and the Lancashire County Record Office, were helpful in answering postal enquiries and in furnishing material: I am more than grateful to them. Austin Woolrych's *Battles of the English Civil War* was the springboard for my work. This first-rate book has stood the test of time remarkably well, and where I disagree with Professor Woolrych I do so at my considerable peril. Mr Richard Saxton, following in the footsteps of his illustrious ancestor, drew my maps. The portraits of the various leaders are reproduced by courtesy of the Mansell Collection; both the Buck engraving of Preston, and Charles Cattermole's painting of the battle are in the Harris Museum and Art Gallery. Finally, I must pay tribute to the continued good humour of my wife Lizie and my daughters Jessica and Corinna who, I suspect, would prefer that I spent less time in the Seventeenth Century and more in the Twentieth.

Richard Holmes
Alton
April 1985

5

Preston 1648

Preston was a sprawling encounter battle fought, on 17-19 August 1648, between a Parliamentarian army commanded by Oliver Cromwell, and a mixed force of English Royalists and Scots "Engagers" under the Duke of Hamilton. It was the decisive battle of the Second Civil War, and stands as a lasting example of the superiority of a small and cohesive army with a talented and experienced commander over a larger, less united force with an indecisive leader.

The Second Civil War flickered into life from the embers of the First, which ended, in effect, with the surrender of Charles I to the Scots in the late spring of 1646. True, a few Royalist fortresses still held out, but the surrender of Pendennis and Raglan castles in August left only Harlech in Royalist hands, and this stronghold, after an epic defence, fell on 13 March 1647. Nevertheless, the king's cause seemed far from lost: many of his leading supporters had fled abroad, and the young Prince Charles and his mother, Henrietta Maria, had taken refuge in France, where they provided a focus for Royalist aspirations.

The king had surrendered to the Scots, rather than to the Parliamentarians, quite deliberately. He hoped that the Scots could be persuaded to aid him against his English enemies in return for political and religious concessions, and in mid-July the Scots submitted their terms—the Newcastle Propositions—to the monarch. In February 1638 a powerful group of the king's Scottish opponents had drawn up the National Covenant, a document which bound those who subscribed to it to maintain "the true Reformed Religion". The Covenant was signed by thousands of Scots in the months that followed, and it became the cornerstone of Scottish nationalism over the next troubled decade. By the terms of the Newcastle Propositions, Charles himself was to take the Covenant, and agree to the imposition of Presbyterianism upon England. Many prominent Royalists were specifically exempted from pardon, and others were to be fined. The king, protesting that he would abandon neither his religion nor his friends, could not bring himself to buy Scottish support at such a price, and in January 1647, after the Scots had received the first instalment of their payment for assistance to Parliament's forces during the war, he was handed over to the English and escorted to Holmby House in Northamptonshire.

Charles's position was still not hopeless. There had always been tensions amongst his enemies: with the war at an end, dissention was rife in the Parliamentarian ranks, with increasing friction between the conservative Presbyterians and the more extreme Independents. Charles was a prisoner but he was also king, and, while some of his wartime opponents favoured a settlement which would end the monarchy altogether—and, so some firebrands argued, bring about far-reaching social and political changes—the majority sought a compromise which would preserve most of the political fabric of pre-war England, making the king a constitutional monarch with limited powers.

The New Model Army, under its commander-in-chief, General Sir Thomas Fairfax, had been the instrument of Parliamentarian victory, and its role in the search for a settlement was scarcely less important than its wartime task. Parliament's attempts to disband the army before its arrears had been paid, and without an acceptable political settlement, provoked growing dissatisfaction. A General Council of the Army was set up, containing the generals, as well as two officers and two other representatives from each regiment. The army concentrated in East Anglia: its "Declaration" of 14 June proclaimed its determination to oppose Parliament in defence of its rights, and it advanced on London. A mutiny by the ill-assorted rabble called out by Parliament in its defence persuaded the leading Independents to flee to meet the army which entered the capital on 6 August.

There followed a three-month period of intense political debate, within the army as well as outside it, which culminated in the General Council being broken up and the regimental representatives—some of whom had become increasingly immoderate in their views—being ordered back to their units. Two regiments mutined, but were restored to obedience by the prompt action of the army's second-in-command, Lieutenant-General Oliver Cromwell.

In this period of turmoil, with army and Parliament striving to agree upon a settlement, Charles had been playing his own role in the fatal drama which was to lead his supporters to defeat at Preston and bring him to the block. On 31 May,

7

Cornet George Joyce had removed the king from Holmby House after the Parliamentary commissioners there had departed precipitately. The king was lodged at Hampton Court, but, on 11 November, the day that the General Council broke up, he escaped and made his way to Carisbrooke Castle on the Isle of Wight, where the governor, Colonel Robert Hammond, kept him in honourable custody. Charles negotiated simultaneously with Parliament and the Scots, and on 26 December he concluded the "Engagement" with the latter. He undertook to introduce Presbyterianism into England for a trial period of three years, and to suppress other sects—"Anti-trinitarians, Anabaptists, Antinominians, Arminians, Familists, Brownists, Seperatists, Independents, Libertines and Seekers." In return, the Scots were to issue a declaration affirming the king's rights, and would champion these by force of arms. The Engagement duly signed, Charles rejected Parliament's most recent negotiating document, and Parliament replied with the Vote of No Addresses, forbidding further discussions.

Fighting broke out in the spring. Discontented and unpaid Parliamentarian troops declared for the king in Wales, northern Royalists seized Berwick and Carlisle, their Kentish comrades took Dartford, Deptford and Rochester, there was a mutiny in the Fleet, and the war in Ireland took a turn for the worse when Lord Inchiquin changed sides and declared for the king and the Scots. Fairfax, who had recently succeeded to his father's barony, sent Cromwell to deal with the rebels in Wales, while he marched against the Kentish Royalists, beating them at Maidstone and pursuing the survivors to Colchester in Essex, where the local Royalists were also in arms. Having failed in two attempts to take the city by storm, Fairfax settled down for a formal seige, uncomfortably aware that Cromwell was similarly engaged before Pembroke. Meanwhile, to the north, Major-General John Lambert faced Sir Marmaduke Langdale's Royalists and braced himself to meet the imminent Scottish invasion.

The Scots, having concluded their Engagement with Charles, wrote to Parliament demanding that negotiations with the King should be reopened, all Englishmen should take the Covenant and the army—"that army of sectaries"—should be disbanded. Parliament rejected these terms, and the Scots prepared to invade. The

Scottish army had been a formidable military instrument in the recent past. During the First Civil War it had operated successfully in England: at Marston Moor on 2 July 1644 the Scottish commander, Alexander Leslie, Earl of Leven, who had served under the Swedish King Gustavus Adolphus in the Thirty Years War, was responsible for drawing up the Allied army and launching it into the attack which was to win the battle.

But in 1648 the Scots had serious problems. In the first place, there was a sharp political division within Scotland. The powerful Earl of Argyll and many of the clergy firmly opposed the war. The English Royalists had not taken the Covenant: indeed, some of them were Roman Catholics, alongside whom no good Presbyterian should fight. The Duke of Hamilton's party—the Engagers—enjoyed widespread support amongst the nobility and gentry, who resented the Kirk's increased political power, and wanted the king back to buttress their own authority. At a lower level, there was war-weariness amongst men for whom these major political issues counted for little. Few volunteered cheerfully for a distant war in a doubtful cause. Even those who supported the war admitted that it was cripplingly expensive. The eminent Presbyterian divine Robert Baillie complained that:

Never an army was so great a charge to the country, the foot-soldiers for levy-money, clothes and arms, costing generally one hundred pounds, the horsemen being three hundred marks, and their free quarter, being an unlimited plundering of many very good pious people.[1]

Rivalries amongst the Scottish leaders made the appointment of senior officers a contentious issue. Old Alexander Leslie would not serve, and David Leslie, another of the many Scots with substantial military experience, was subjected to what Baillie called "threats and promises" to dissuade him from taking command. The post of general went instead to James, Duke of Hamilton, a forty-two year old politician whose only experience of war had been an abortive expedition to Germany in 1634. The historian S. R. Gardiner wrote that Hamiltons's "character seems to have been devoid of intellectual or moral strength."[2] Given the state of Scottish politics in the late 1640s it would have taken a cleverer man than Hamilton to have kept his footing in the turmoil, and, as we shall see, he did not lack physical courage. Nevertheless, his inexperience and weak character made him a poor choice for supreme command.

Hamilton's lieutenant-general (second-in-command) was James Livingstone, Earl of Callander. In contrast to his general, Callander had a sound military record, having served with distinction in the Low Countries, and in England during the First Civil War. Although Hamilton and Callander were both members of the anti-Argyll faction, they were personal enemies. Robert Baillie admitted that: "Both of them to that time had been opposed to the employment of either... and each offered to mar the employment of the other." Callander had already shown himself reluctant to accept a subordinate position, and he chafed at being under Hamilton's command. "Callander was doubly to be blamed," wrote Sir James Turner, "first for his conduct, for that was inexcusable, and next for his reproaching the Duke for that whereof himself was guilty."[3]

The remaining senior officers were wiser choices. John Middleton, later Earl of Middleton, was lieutenant-general of the horse. He had begun his military career as a pikeman in Hepburn's Regiment in the French service, and had served as a lieutenant-general in the Parliamentarian army during the First Civil War, resigning when the army was remodelled. His infantry counterpart, lieutenant-general of the foot, was William Baillie, once a colonel of foot under Gustavus. The adjutant-general of the Scottish army—as close as that force came to the post of chief of staff—was James Turner, another veteran of Swedish service, described by Bishop Burnet as:

naturally fierce, but he was mad when he was drunk, and that was very often... he was a learned man, but had always been in armies, and knew no rule but to obey orders.[4]

The appointment of senior officers and the raising of the Scottish army all consumed valuable time. Had the Scots marched south in the spring of 1648, at the very time that the English Royalists rose, then Fairfax's resources would have been stretched to snapping point. But May and June were spent raising troops. There was active resistance to the general levy: Turner, recruiting in the Glasgow area, took to billeting soldiers on recalcitrant inhabitants to quell their opposition, and there was an armed rising in Ayrshire, which culminated in a skirmish on Mauchline Moor. In late June Robert Baillie wrote in despair that: "Our affairs here have. . . had a great progress, but no inch to the better; all appearance of any possibility to agree daily does more and more vanish."[5]

The plight of the Scots and their opponents alike was worsened by the weather. It was, as all contemporary accounts emphasise, an atrocious summer, the worst in living memory. The country was pelted by gales and torrential rain. A Scottish officer complained that "there were such deluges of rain not only over England but all over Europe, that every brook was a river, which made the march very heavy to both horse and foot," while Captain Samuel Birch of the Lancashire foot agreed that it was as "miserable time for soldiers as I have seen at any time."[6]

Such weather had a profound effect on Seventeenth-Century armies. Roads were unmetalled—minor roads were often scarcely better than cart-tracks—and the rain turned them into quagmires: wagons sunk up to their axles in the mud, and horse and foot splashed glumly through the mire. About two-thirds of the infantry on both sides were musketeers, equipped with the muzzle-loading matchlock musket. This weapon had a fighting range of perhaps 150 yards, and he would be a skilled man indeed who could get off more than one shot a minute. The matchlock's chief disadvantage was that it depended upon the match—a glowing length of saltpetre-soaked cord—to ignite its charge. In rainy weather it was difficult to keep powder dry and matches alight: Turner recalled that the summer "was so excessively rainy and wet that it was not possible for us to keep one musket of ten fixed all the time we were in a body in England."[7] A fortunate few may have carried the more reliable flintlock—we know that at least one Scots regiment was equipped with flintlocks at the battle of Dunbar in September 1650—but for most of this period the "firelock" was issued only to those infantrymen guarding the artillery, where lengths of sputtering match amongst the powder-barrels would have been decidedly dangerous.

The remainder of the foot were pikemen, carrying a pike whose regulation length was 18 feet, although in practice 16 feet seems to have been more common. Pikemen had traditionally worn helmet, breast- and backplate, with long tassets covering their thighs. Although armour gave its wearer useful protection when the infantry came to "push of pike", it was an encumberance on the march, and by 1648 it was usually lightened by the omission of the tassets, or even discarded altogether.

Armour was also losing its popularity amongst the cavalry. Although the New Model's troopers should have worn breast- and backplate over their stout leather buff-coats, some of them probably fought without armour at Preston. Cavalrymen on both sides wore helmets—some of the Scots horse wore the old-fashioned "steill bonnett", the burgonet, and the lobstertail pot was by no means confined to the New Model—or felt hats with a metal "spider" inside them. A well-armed trooper carried both sword and wheel-lock pistol, and the First Civil War had demonstrated the importance of charging home to fire pistols at close quarters before falling to with the sword. The Scots equipped some of their cavalry, especially those raised in the borders, with the lance, a deadly weapon in the hands of a skilled man. Although the Scottish cavalry had a poor reputation, largely on account of the small size of its horses, Scots lancers were no mean adversaries, as they were to demonstrate at Preston.

A few horsemen carried wheel-lock carbines, though these did not become a general issue till the 1650s. At Preston they were probably used by Parliamentarian officers who had obtained them privately: when a mutineer was hunted down in May 1649, the corporal who shot him did so with his colonel's carbine. Dragoons were something of a hybrid, wearing no armour, and equipped with sword and musket. They were expected to operate with an army's vanguard, securing bridges and other defiles, and, like the infantry's musketeers, they could be used to line hedges in enclosed country.

There had been an increasing degree of uniformity in military dress during the First Civil War, and by 1648 the infantry of the New Model wore red coats. There was more variation amongst the Scots, although the sombre and practical "hodden grey" was widely worn amongst horse and foot. The flat blue cloth bonnet was very popular with the Scottish foot, and was worn almost universally by them on the march, though most Scots pikemen probably replaced it with a helmet in battle, tucking the bonnet under their belts.

The regiment was the standard unit of organization for the horses and foot on both sides in 1648. Details of establishment varied between armies. Foot regiments of the New Model had a strength of 1,200 men, divided into ten companies. The colonel's company—commanded in practice by his captain-lieutenant—was 200 strong, the lieutenant-colonel's 160 and the major's 140: the remaining companies, captains' commands, numbered 100 men apiece. The New Model's horse regiments had 600 men each, divided into six equal troops. The Scots and the English Royalists had similar organizations. However, while Parliamentarian units were generally up to strength—Captain Samuel Birch's company of foot, raised in Lancashire, had a paid strength of one captain, one lieutenant, one ensign, two sergeants, two drummers, four corporals and 135 private soldiers—the Scots and their allies were less generously recruited.[8] As Sir Philip Musgrave admits, the eight regiments of Royalist foot that met near Carlisle in May numbered only 3,000 men between them.[9]

When Hamilton crossed the border on 8 July his army was still in bad order. He had some 9,000 men under command, two-thirds of them infantry. His foot regiments were mostly at only half their regulation strength, and their pikemen and musketeers were largely untrained. The horse were scarcely better: although "the best mounted that ever Scotland set out, yet most of the troopers were raw and undisciplined."[10] There were many seasoned officers with the army, but most of them became involved in factional politics. "The inferior officers stood all divided," wrote one officer, "according as their affections led them, either to the general or the lieutenant-general, and thus the army modelled." There was a shortage of ammunition and draught-horses, and the army's artillery had been left behind in Scotland. The need to procure horses and drivers locally, allied to indiscipline and a non-existent commissariat, soon led to plundering. "They have taken forth of divers families all," complained a Lancastrian,

the very racken crocks and pot hooks; they have driven away all the beasts, sheep and horses... They tell the people they must have their houses too... Their usage of some women is extremely abominable, and of men very barbarous...[11]

So many women accompanied Hamilton's army that many of the inhabitants believed that the Scots had come to stay, which scarcely encouraged the numerous northerners who were Royalists at heart.

There was also marked friction between the Scots and their English allies. The Royalists had hoped that the Scots would move South in the Spring, in concert with the Royalist risings throughout England, and the leaders of the northern Royalists, Sir Marmaduke Langdale and Sir Philip Musgrave, who seized Carlisle and Berwick in late April, begged for speedy help. On 14 June Musgrave wrote to Hamilton's brother, the Earl of Lanark:

Sir Marmaduke Langdale. . . desires your very speedy assistance in this business of so great concernment for his Majesty's affairs (according to your Lordship's engagement). Most of the prime gentry from the North of England. . . are resolutely bent to hazard their lives in this present action, which we doubt not will move your Lordship to a more effectual consideration of us.[12]

Far from receiving prompt assistance, Musgrave had to travel to Edinburgh to answer charges that there were papists amongst his followers.

There was undoubtedly some substance to the Kirk's fears. Sir Marmaduke Langdale, the Royalist commander, came from an old Roman Catholic Yorkshire family. In February 1643 he had raised a foot regiment in the East Riding, but it was as a cavalry leader that he had made his reputation. In February 1643 he beat Colonel Rossiter at Melton Mowbray and raised the seige of Pontefract, but later that year he commanded the left wing at Naseby and was roundly defeated. However, although there were some Catholics in the Royalist army, the overwhelming majority of the northern Catholics, fearing that direct participation in the war would only worsen their plight, kept their Royalist sympathies to themselves, and stayed at home.

In May-June 1648 Langdale's little army, 3,000 foot and 700 ill-armed horse from Cumberland and Westmoreland, with 500 good horse from other counties, waited impatiently for the Scots, watched by a small force under the twenty-eight year old Major-General John Lambert. Lambert had 3,500 men of his own, reinforced by Ralph Ashton, Colonel-General of Lancashire, commanding some 1,000 foot and

300 horse of the Lancashire levies.

During the First Civil War Lancashire, in common with other English counties, had been "by the sword divided". Most Lancastrians, especially those living in the northern part of the county, were probably pro-Royalist, and several of the MPs for the county's constituencies had declared for King rather than Parliament. James Stanley, 7th Earl of Derby, was the most prominent Royalist leader in the county, supported by other local magnates like Sir Thomas Tyldesley of Myserscough Lodge near Garstang and Sir Gilbert Hoghton, one of whose seats was Walton Hall, just South of Preston. Ralph Ashton, a moderate Presbyterian and one of the two MPs for Lancashire, was the leading Parliamentarian in the county and, assisted by his three colonels, Alexander Rigby, Richard Shuttleworth and John Moore, he had played a distinguished part during the First Civil War. On 17 May 1648 the Commons had ordered Ashton to recruit men to meet the expected Scottish invasion, and by early June he had 1,500 Foot and 1,200 Horse under arms. Although not all Ashton's men were present with Lambert, the Lancashire contingent was a valuable asset to the Parliamentarian force, not only providing it with a wealth of local knowledge—especially important in an era when maps were scarce—but also, as we shall see, making a potent contribution to its fighting effectiveness.

Fairfax had intended that Lambert should mask Langdale until the main body of the New Model could march North. But he himself remained bogged down before Colchester, while Cromwell was stuck fast at Pembroke, leaving Lambert to face not only Langdale but also the growing power of the Scots.

It was fortunate for the Parliamentarian cause that Hamilton continued to move with painful slowness, and that Lambert was an officer of outstanding ability. Hamilton paused for six days at Carlisle, and on 14 July his cavalry caught Lambert's near Penrith, but the foot were too far back to bring about a general engagement. Three days later he attacked Lambert at Appleby. "The Scots fell upon us before we were aware," acknowledged Captain Birch,

Our horse being—the greatest part—absent: drew up our horse guards within our centres and quarters of foot, drew out parties which kept them off from us till night, and made divers works, but by day break in the morning we marched away. I had the rearguard of the foot with Major Greenlish.[13]

Hamilton was still in no mood for pursuit: instead, he halted at Kirkby Thore for the rest of the month, waiting for reinforcements from Scotland. The regiments which arrived were ill-trained and under-recruited, bringing the duke's strength up to 10,000 foot and 4,000 horse, together with Langdale's 3,000 foot and 1,200 horse. He also received word that Sir George Monro, with 2,100 foot and 1,200 horse from the Scots army in Ulster, was on his way to join him. Monro's men would have been a useful addition to the duke's army, "for they were resolute and well trained."[14] However, they had to cross from Ireland at night in tiny vessels to avoid two Parliamentarian warships, and were vilified by the populace as they marched through Galloway to join Hamilton.

Lambert, meanwhile, had concentrated around Bowes and Barnard Castle, equally ready to oppose the Scots if they crossed the Pennines to move down into Yorkshire, or to hang onto their flank if they remained west of the Pennines and marched through Lancashire. On 26th July the Scots attacked Lambert's men on Stainmore but, having dislodged them from the pass, made no attempt to exploit their success. This is probably because Hamilton's council of war decided, for the time being at least, to advance through Lancashire. The duke set off from Kirkby Thore on 31 July, reached Kendal the next day, and stayed there for a week, hoping for further reinforcements, and still perilously short of transport, supplies and ammunition. Sir George Monro, several days' march ahead of his men, met Hamilton at Kendal. His appearance was a mixed blessing, for it was immediately obvious that Sir George was gripped by the spirit of factionalism which afflicted so many Scottish senior officers. He made it clear that he "had no mind to take orders either from Callander or Baillie," so Hamilton ordered him to wait at Kirkby Lonsdale, with his own veterans and the English infantry regiments of Musgrave and Sir Thomas Tyldesley, to escort the cannon when they eventually arrived from Scotland.[15] This decision was probably inspired by political rather than military motives, for it was clear to Hamilton that if Monro accompanied the main body of the army there would be trouble between him and Callander.

The rest of the northern Royalists, under Langdale's command, were now based on Settle. Sir Marmaduke considered striking out to relieve a Royalist garrison in Pontefract, and unsuccessfully attempted to persuade the governor of Skipton Castle to betray it to him. Lambert had conformed with his movements by falling back first to Richmond, then to Ripon and, on 7 August, to Knaresborough.

But by the end of the first week in August the strategic situation, once so promising for the Scots and the Royalists, had been transformed. Although Colchester still held out, risings elsewhere had been crushed and the fleet had been restored to obedience. Pembroke Castle fell on 11 July, and Cromwell set off at once for Yorkshire, sending much of his cavalry on ahead and marching with three regiments of foot and one of horse, with a few dragoons. He reached Leicester on 1 August, his men footsore and weary, as one of them graphically described:

Our marches long, and want of shoes and stockings gives discouragement to our soldiers, having received no pay these many months to buy them, nor can any procure unless we plunder, which was never heard of by any under the Lieutenant General's conduct nor will be, though they march barefoot, which many have done, since our advance from Wales. [16]

The arrival of 2,500 pairs of shoes from Northampton and 2,500 pairs of stockings from Coventry, which probably reached Cromwell at Nottingham on 5 August, did wonders for morale, and on the 8th he was at Doncaster. Cromwell's cavalry had already reached Lambert, and his main body, after a three-day wait at Doncaster for artillery to arrive from Hull—a delay Cromwell used to help the besigers of Pontefract—met Lambert between Knaresborough and Wetherby on the 12th.

Cromwell's army—his own regiments from Wales, Lambert's force and Ashton's Lancastrians—had perhaps 8,600 men available to take the field, for Scarborough had just risen in revolt and two regiments had to be left to cover it. Captain John Hodgson of Bright's Regiment of Foot had been with Lambert from the outset, and he reported that: "We were then betwixt eight or nine thousand; a fine smart army, and fit for action." [17]

Hamilton's army was infinitely more numerous—though contemporary estimates of 21-24,000 were probably inaccurate—but far less ready for battle. The duke had reached Hornby on the 9th, and remained there for another five days. It was at Hornby on the 13th that his council of war met to consider the army's future operations. There were two courses open to Hamilton. He could remain in Lancashire, and march into Cheshire and North Wales, taking Manchester, which he hoped would declare for the King, before linking up with Welsh Royalists under Lord Byron. Alternatively, he could cross the Pennines, marching by way of Skipton, and advance through Yorkshire, making for London by the most direct route and fighting any army in his path.

There are conflicting accounts of the debate which led to the council's decision, and the discussion cannot be reconstructed with absolute certainty. Bishop Burnet had access to a well-placed Scottish source, but his book, written with the declared aim of rescuing the reputation of Hamilton and his brother, is less reliable than Turner's eyewitness account. Langdale was also present, having ridden over from Settle to warn Hamilton that Lambert's forces had been strengthened, although at this stage he seems, not unreasonably, to have had little idea of the proximity of Cromwell. He tells us that Hamilton decided to march on Preston, "where (his army being numerous in foot) he might have the greater advantage upon his enemy in those enclosed countries." Turner suggests that Callander was indifferent, Middleton was for Yorkshire and Baillie for Lancashire. He himself favoured Yorkshire:

and for this reason only, that I understood Lancashire was a close country, full of ditches and hedges, which was a great advantage the English would have over our raw and undisciplined musketeers; the Parliament's army consisting of disciplined and well-trained soldiers, and excellent firemen; while on the other hand, Yorkshire was a more open country and full of heaths, where we might both make use of our horse, and come sooner to push of pike with our foot.

Turner maintains that Hamilton "was for the Lancashire way" and, though Burnet has Hamilton and Baillie favour Yorkshire and Callander and Langdale Lancashire, Turner takes pains to emphasise Hamilton's determination to choose Lancashire. "Whatever the matter was," declared Turner, "I never saw him tenacious during the time of his command but in that."[18]

THE BATTLE

While the Allied commanders were conferring, Cromwell was on the move. He set off on the 13th, having sent his artillery—which had cost him that three-day delay at Doncaster—into Knaresborough, "because of the difficulty of marching therewith through Craven, and to the end that we might with more expedition attend the enemy's motion."[19] He had reached Skipton on the 14th—when his son Henry, a captain in Harrison's Regiment of Horse, pushed on to drive some of Langdale's troopers out of Gargrave—and arrived at Gisburn on the 15th. Langdale had fallen back down Ribblesdale, with Cromwell close behind. Although there were several clashes between the opposing cavalry, and Cromwell's advance guard captured Colonel Tempest and a party of horse at Waddow near Clitheroe on the 16th, Langdale still failed to identify the presence of Cromwell and his army, and seems not to have sent Hamilton any fresh intelligence to supplement his warning of 13 August.

Cromwell's council of war met on the 16th, three days after Hamilton's, by the roadside at what Cromwell described as Hodder Bridge, on what is now the B6243 just West of Clitheroe. It is, however, more likely, given the nature of the debate at the council, that the discussion took place at Edisford Bridge over the Ribble, just outside Clitheroe. Just as Hamilton's senior officers had to decide which direction their march should take, so Cromwell's council of war faced a choice between two lines of advance. They considered whether to remain South of the Ribble, and march to Whalley that night, before turning westwards to "interpose between the Enemy and his further progress into Lancashire", or to cross the bridge, and stay North of the Ribble and its tributary the Hodder, to bring Hamilton to battle in Preston itself. Believing—wrongly, in the event—that Hamilton would stand his ground around Preston because he was waiting for Monro to come up, and more fundamentally, because "it was thought that to engage the enemy to fight was our business", the council decided to cross the river and press for a battle.[20]

The Scots advanced southwards oblivious to the threat to their flank. Hamilton had been under pressure from his senior officers to "enlarge quarters" so that the army could forage as widely as possible and, uncomfortably aware of the need to live off the country, he permitted a remarkable degree of dispersion. Langdale,

19

visited by Callander as he marched from Clitheroe towards Preston, had been told that the Parliamentarian forces were divided: some were making for Colne, others for Manchester. "This," he thought, "made the Officers of Horse more negligent of repairing to Preston, but quartered wide in the country."[21]

The heavens continued to conspire against the duke and his men. "Our march was much retarded by most rainy and tempestuous weather," wrote Turner, "the elements fighting against us; and by staying for country horses to carry our little ammunition."[22] On the 16th, Callander and Middleton led the cavalry towards Wigan, sixteen miles south of Preston, while the duke, with the main body of the Scottish Foot, was still marching down the present A6 to the north of Preston: the swollen Ribble, not bridged between Walton Bridge and the sea, cut across the Scottish army like a knife.

By now the armies were far closer than either Langdale or Hamilton imagined. Cromwell crossed the Hodder at Lower Hodder Bridge, and camped for the night of Wednesday, 16 August in the grounds of what Captain Hodgson called "Stanyares hall, a papist's house, one Sherburne," and Cromwell, with a keener regard for both spelling and the householder's feelings, termed "Stonyhurst Hall, being Mr Sherburn's house, a place nine miles distant from Preston."[23] Langdale's quarters were only three miles down the valley, and during the night Sir Marmaduke at last recognised that the Parliamentarians were close by in strength. He at once sent a messenger to warn Hamilton, got his men on the move towards Preston, and rode for the town himself. What is unclear, however, is whether Langdale realised that he was in contact with Cromwell's main body or, as seems more probable, he had simply reported that he had encountered the advanced guard of a mixed force of unknown size.

Cromwell sent his advanced guard, 200 horse under Major Smithson and 400 foot under Major Pownall and Captain Hodgson, in pursuit of Langdale without delay, and followed up with the remainder of his force: by late morning this advance guard was in contact with Langdale's outposts between Longridge and Preston. As the smoke of the first shots of the battle rolled out across the sodden moorland, Hamilton's position was still not hopeless. His army was dangerously weakened by the sixteen-mile gap between the leading horse and the main body of the foot, while Monro's Scots and the northern regiments of Musgrave and Tyldesley—4,500 in all—were up near Kirkby Lonsdale, too far to the rear to be of any use that day. Nevertheless, Langdale's 3,000 foot and 600 horse could hold Cromwell for a time, and Hamilton probably had 8-10,000 Scottish foot under his hand around Preston. Cromwell reckoned his own force at 4,000 foot and 2,500 mounted men of the New Model, strengthened by the Lancashire brigade of 1,600 Foot and 500 Horse. Despite his over-extension, the duke enjoyed a numerical advantage in the Preston area, and, as late as midday on the 17th, he still had it in his power to turn it to his advantage.

Langdale's messenger found the Scottish high command already in some confusion. On the 16th Callander had gleaned information of Cromwell's approach—possibly from parties of his horse who had been posted out near Clitheroe. He left the advanced guard under Middleton's command at Wigan and rode back to Preston. Although Callander did not tell the duke all he knew, Hamilton was concerned enough to look for a suitable place to offer battle, finding, on the morning of the 17th, that Preston Moor would not do, because "we... had not ground enough." While Hamilton was on his reconnaissance, Callander ordered Baillie to take the foot across Walton Bridge, and Hamilton returned to find them crossing. At about this time Langdale's galloper arrived, and the duke ordered Baillie to keep the foot on the north side of the bridge, and sent Middleton word to bring the horse back as fast as he could.

Callander at once rode up from the bridge to Preston Moor (in the area where Moor Park now lies), where he found the Hamilton with his guard, the cavalry of the rearguard, and two brigades of foot. He warned the duke that if he accepted battle with horse and foot so widely separated he risked defeat in detail. It was far better, he argued, to get infantry safely across the river and link up with Middleton in order to give battle with a united force the following day. Hamilton, overawed by his experienced subordinate, gave way, and the foot resumed their crossing: the duke himself, with his own horse guard and the rearguard cavalry, remained north of the Ribble, and the two rearmost brigades of Scottish foot marched down to

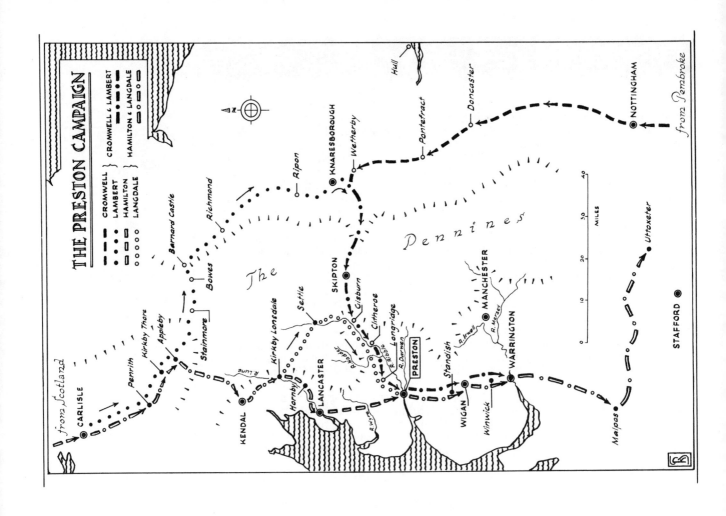

THE PRESTON CAMPAIGN

CROMWELL
LAMBERT } CROMWELL & LAMBERT
HAMILTON
LANGDALE } HAMILTON & LANGDALE

Oliver Cromwell.

Sir Marmaduke Langdale.

The Duke of Hamilton.

Major-General John Lambert.

A Pikeman, from Jacob de Gheyn's drillbook, **The Exercise of Arms,** (The Hague 1607). The soldier is bracing his pike against his foot and drawing his sword in preparation for receiving cavalry. By 1648 the long tassets covering the thighs had generally disappeared, and the baggy breeches had been replaced by more close-fitting garments.

A musketeer, from de Gheyn. He is in the act of firing, and the match, alight at both ends, is clearly visible. Note also the bandolier with charges from the musket and a small flask of priming powder.

Charles Cattermole's painting of the battle. Although Cattermole is wrong on some points of detail (for example he shows a cannon in the left foreground), his painting, looking north to south from a viewpoint near the figure 10 on the Buck engraving, gives a good idea of the battle and a reasonable feel for the ground. Walton church (14 on Buck's print) is in the background on the left, and Walton Hill in the background to the right.

A detail from the 1728 view of Preston from the south by S. and N. Buck. The view is taken from behind the Scots' position on Walton Hill. Walton Hall can be seen in the right foreground, with Walton Bridge crossing the Ribble behind it. The main London road curls around the houses on the far side of the bridge, and stoneygate Lane runs straight from the bridge to the town. The Swill Brook, its prominent valley shown clearly, runs into the Ribble just above the left-hand sailing vessel. The tower of Preston Town Hall can be seen on the skyline at the extreme left. Note the excellent cover on the northern side of Walton Bridge, and the exposed Flats on its southern side.

The Earl of Callander.

The old Lower Hodder Bridge. Cromwell crossed the Hodder (from left to right) here on 16 August 1648, possibly using an earlier bridge.

Watery Lane, the unguarded track to the right rear of Langdale's position. It was down this lane that Assheton's men marched to reach Walton Bridge.

The Eaves Brook, looking from Ribbleton Lane towards Ribbleton Moor. The Parliamentarians attacked from left to right.

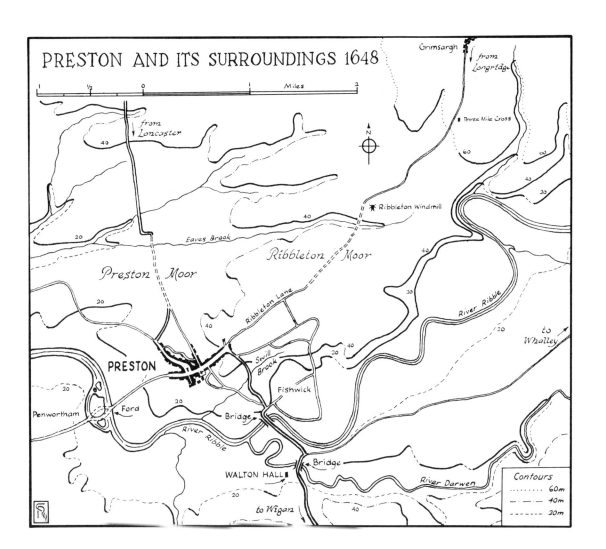

PRESTON AND ITS SURROUNDINGS 1648

Miles

from Loncaster

Grimsargh

from Longridge

Three Mile Cross

60

40

20

40

20

Ribbleton Windmill

Eaves Brook

40

Ribbleton Moor

Preston Moor

40

20

River Ribble

40

20

20

Ribbleton Lane

40

20

to Whalley

PRESTON

Swill Brook

Fishwick

20

Penwortham

Ford

20

Bridge

River Ribble

Bridge

WALTON HALL

River Darwen

20

to Wigan

40

Contours	
·········	60m
— · —	40m
— — —	20m

cover the bridge.

Prompt action—swinging the foot to the east to join Langdale, and recalling the horse—very much as Hamilton had initially ordered—might yet have given the duke a chance, if not of victory, then at least of averting catastrophe. But, even when Langdale himself joined Hamilton on Preston Moor, the Scottish general paid little attention to his warnings, and, Callander's urgings still fresh in his mind, announced that he intended to march on to Wigan.

Once again the sources leave some room for doubt. Burnet's account takes a steadfastly pro-Hamilton line, while Langdale's own relation of events is scarcely unbiased. It may be that Langdale still did not realise that he was facing Cromwell's main body and failed to put his case forcefully enough. But it is more likely that Hamilton, his feelings towards Langdale coloured by that distrust of allies which had been such a marked feature of the campaign, thought that the Yorkshireman was overreacting and was dealing only with Lambert's force, and believed that the English contingent should be able to hold its own while the Scots crossed the bridge. At least one contemporary thought that sheer malice contributed to the duke's decision, reporting that when Hamilton was told of Cromwell's attack on Langdale, he replied: "let them alone: the English dogs are but killing one another."[24]

Langdale rode back to his little army as it prepared for battle astride the Longridge-Preston road—the modern B6243—just over two miles from Preston market-place. The road dipped sharply to cross the Eaves Brook, and the defile was, as Cromwell put it, "very deep and ill." Langdale had left a small screening force about a mile further out towards Longridge, and had deployed his main body behind the Eaves Brook. Ribbleton Moor stretched out from Langdale's right flank towards the river, but Sir Marmaduke had made good use of the many small enclosures which were then a feature of the area north of the moor, lining the hedges with his musketeers. The ground was so wet that cavalry could operate only with difficulty, and the lane was particularly muddy in the area of the brook. Hodgson, skirmishing down from Longridge with the Parliamentarian advanced guard, thought that the Royalists were drawn up "very formidably", and even the doughty Cromwell felt that the miry lane, hedged enclosures and sodden ground made matters extremely difficult.[25]

Cromwell pushed his advanced guard into battle as quickly as he could: so fast, indeed, that Hodgson complained that many of their men had not yet come up. Smithson's horse went straight down the lane, and a counter-attack by Scottish lancers temporarily threw them back. Hodgson, with the foot of the advanced guard, was also heavily engaged:

we drew over a little common, and came to a ditch [almost certainly the Eaves Brook], *and the enemy let fly at us (a company of Langdale's men that was newly raised). They shot at the skies, which did so encourage our men, that they were willing to venture upon any attempt; and the major orders me to march to the next hedge, and I bid him order the men to follow me, and there drew out a small party; and we came up to the hedge end, and the enemy, many of them, threw down their arms and run to their party, where was their stand of pikes, and a great body of colours.*[26]

Hodgson's account suggests that Langdale had covered the brook with the fire of musketeers, with the main body of his army amongst the hedges atop the slope behind it.

While his advanced guard pinned Langdale to his position, Cromwell formed his army for the attack in "as good a posture as the ground would bear." He ordered two regiments of horse, Harrison's and his own, to charge straight down the lane. To the right of the lane Reade's, Dean's and Pride's regiments of foot advanced to clear the hedges, with the infantry regiments of Bright and Fairfax on the left of the road. Thornhaugh's and Twistleton's regiments of horse supported the attack on the right, one regiment remained in reserve for the lane, and the remaining horse buttressed the foot on the left. Ashton's Lancasterians were in reserve for this phase of the battle.[27]

Dean's and Pride's regiments on the Parliamentarian right outflanked the Royalists, and so saw little action, but Cromwell kept them in place, no doubt fearing that he himself might be outflanked if Hamilton marched straight to Langdale's assistance. Across the rest of the front, the battle was both long and bitter, Langdale's men putting up, as Cromwell frankly admitted, "very stiff and sturdy resistance," particularly on the Parliamentarian left.[28]

Cromwell noted that the Royalists tended to "shog" gradually to the south-west, edging back towards the Ribble bridge, lessening their resistance north of the road but putting up a heavy defence south of it. So fierce was their resistance that the Parliamentarian first line could not overcome it, and Ashton's men had to be committed to battle. Hodgson, now mounted on a captured horse, had been ordered forward to his colonel, Bright, "deeply engaged both in front and flank" on the left of the lane. Hodgson rode forward and found:

nothing but fire and smoke; and I met Major-General Lambert coming off on foot, who had been with his brother Bright; and coming to him, I told him where his danger lay, on his left wing chiefly. He ordered me to fetch up the Lancashire regiment; and God brought me off, both my horse and myself. The bullets flew freely; then was the heat of battle that day. I came down to the muir, where I met with Major Jackson, that belonged to Ashton's regiment, and about three hundred men were come up; I ordered him to march, but he said he would not, till his men were come up. A serjeant, belonging to them, asked me, where they should march? I showed him the party he was to fight; and he, like a true bred Englishman, marched, and I caused the soldiers to follow him; which presently fell upon the enemy, and, losing that wing, the whole army gave ground and fled.[29]

The attack of the Lancastrians was decisive. Langdale's men fell back into Preston, pursued by four troops of Cromwell's regiment and the whole of Harrison's regiment, who "cleared the streets." A small lane (now Watery Lane) led from the right rear of Langdale's position towards the Ribble, and this had not been secured either by Langdale's men or by the Scots. Ashton's Lancastrians pressed on down it, and swung south-west to reach the Ribble at Walton Bridge. This phase of the battle ended with almost total destruction of Langdale's force. Many of the Royalists lay out amongst the hedges, or in the mud of the lane, and most of the survivors sought refuge in the town.

It was by now late afternoon. Cromwell believed that his battle against Langdale lasted for four hours: Langdale with pardonable exaggeration, thought six, and a contemporary news-sheet stated that the crucial part of the action, after Langdale's outposts had been driven in and Cromwell's main attack had been launched against the Royalist position behind the Eaves brook, went on for an hour. Even if Cromwell's main body had got under arms at Stonyhurst Hall at first light, his army, marching along a single narrow road, cannot have deployed for battle much before midday, and it was probably 4.00 pm before Langdale's men at last gave way. Both friend and foe alike paid tribute to the dogged bravery of Sir Marmaduke and his soldiers, and their courage brought Hamilton more time than he might have expected.

Langdale complained bitterly that Scottish support would have swung the balance of the battle in his favour: "if they had sent me 1000 foot to have flanked the enemy I doubt not the day had been ours."[30] The Scots, for their part, protested that Sir Marmaduke "was well nigh totally routed before we knew that it was Cromwell who attacked us."[31] There is a measure of truth in both statements. Langdale did indeed have every reason to hope that Hamilton, some two miles from the battlefield, with both horse and foot at his disposal, would support him. Hamilton, for his part, may still have been unsure that he had to contend with the main Parliamentarian army under Cromwell himself.

However, the balance of the evidence tends to tell against the duke. While the fighting was still in progress, he sent Sir Lewis Dyve to liaise with Langdale. Sir Marmaduke told Dyve that he was facing the whole of Cromwell's army, and urgently demanded support, as well as fresh supplies of powder and shot. Hamilton sent a few lancers early on—it was they who rebuffed Major Smithson in the lane. Later, recognising that the English were "sore put to it, Cromwell gaining hedge upon hedge of them", ordered Turner to send some foot—700 were in fact dispatched—and some much-needed ammunition. Some of Hamilton's advisers realised how important it was that Langdale should be supported. Sir James Hamilton pressed the point, and was allowed to set off with a party of cavalry, but he encountered Callander, who, protesting that Sir James—a gentleman volunteer in Hamilton's troop of horse—enjoyed no formal command authority, ordered him to rejoin the duke.

By late afternoon Hamilton had missed his chance. Langdale's force had ceased to exist: Cromwell's cavalry were already in Churchgate (now Church Street), and Ashton's men were making for Walton Bridge by way of Watery Lane. The duke himself had remained on Preston Moor with his own guard and the rearguard horse: he ordered the latter to escape to the north and join Monro, and they made off with Parliamentarian cavalry behind them. The pursuit went on for ten miles, and about 500 of the retreating horse were taken. The duke, to his credit, strove to rejoin his foot, all of whom—save a few stragglers in the town—had now crossed Walton Bridge. Accompanied only by a few gentlemen, Langdale and Turner amongst them, and his guard, Hamilton tried to cross the Ribble at a ford below the bridge, but found it impassable. Two troops of Cromwell's horse attacked the general's party. Turner tried to persuade some musketeers to drive them off, but the shaken infantry would not stand. Hamilton led three charges against the Parliamentarians, driving them back long enough for his party to escape from the town, and to swim the Ribble to Penwortham.

Hamilton and his entourage made their way onto Walton Hill, where Baillie had deployed his foot amongst the hedges and enclosures around Walton Hall. Meanwhile, the two brigades holding the bridge were heavily attacked by Ashton's foot, moving up from Watery Lane, and by Fairfax's regiment of foot, which (having been on the extreme left of Cromwell's line during the battle against Langdale) probably followed the same route. The Parliamentarians were later joined by some troops who had marched through the town, dealing with sporadic opposition en route—isolated Scots or Royalist fugitives seem to have offered brief resistance on the line of the Swill Brook, near the present Larkhill Convent—and reaching the bridge by way of Stoneygate Lane. The attackers, firing from the cover of the houses and enclosures on the rising ground north of the bridge, steadily gained the upper hand. Callander strove to redress the balance, and ordered 600 musketeers forward to support their comrades at the bridge, but they came under heavy fire as they crossed the open ground—The Flats—between the Ribble and the Darwen, and could make no progress. The Scots at the bridge fought with commendable determination, and held their position for two hours, but at length they were thrust back at push of pike. Captain Samuel Birch was in the forefront of the action.

I had charge of the Lancashire brigade's forlorn (vanguard); my lieutenant had the charge of my division of musketeers, my ensign, by command of General Ashton, led the pikes and colours up against the defenders on Ribble Bridge and beat them off; almost all my officers marked, none killed, divers soldiers shot and hurt, some very dangerously, most performed very well. Blessed be God for his great deliverance.[32]

The parliamentarians followed up the retreat, taking the Darwen bridge and driving in the Scottish outposts on Walton Hill. The Scots now suffered a further misfortune, for their baggage-wagons had been taken safely across the bridges, but were in front of the main infantry lines on Walton Hill. Their hastily-pressed civilian drivers seized the opportunity to take their horses and escape, and in the last hour of daylight Hamilton's wagons were captured and dragged down the slope. The day ended with what was almost a symbolic accident: one of the wagons overturned, spilling Hamilton's silver plate onto the ground.

Cromwell spent the night in Preston, with as many of his men as he could find quarters in the town. He had every reason to feel satisfied with the day's work, estimating that the allies had lost 4-5,000 weapons, 1,000 killed and 4,000 prisoners, but took immediate steps to press his advantage. He held the bridges over the Darwen and the Ribble, and his outposts at the foot of Walton Hill watched the Scots. He suspected that it was in fact the main body of the Scottish cavalry that his men had chased towards Lancaster, and he feared that Hamilton would try to break back north, crossing the Ribble upstream of Preston, to join them. Accordingly, he ordered some of Ashton's men who had been left behind at Whalley to secure the bridge at Great Mitton, where they would be joined by seven troops of horse from Clitheroe.

Hamilton held a council of war in the rainy darkness of Walton Hill. Callander, who, as lieutenant-general, should by tradition have spoken last, opened the debate by recommending that they should break contact under cover of night, and fall back to meet Middleton, who should by now be on his way up from Wigan. Other senior officers agreed, only Baillie and Turner arguing in favour of holding their strong position and fighting it out there. Hamilton fell in with what Turner called the "shameful resolution" of the majority, and ordered a "drumless march"—a covert withdrawal.[33] It was a fatal decision. Inexperienced though the Scots were, they had already shown that they could fight doggedly enough in defence. A night march in the rain, with empty bellies, down bad roads with an enemy close behind is likely to tax the morale of more seasoned troops, and its effect on Hamilton's raw levies was understandably catastrophic. But worse was to come. Because the drivers had fled with their horses, the surviving wagons could not be moved. The musketeers were therefore ordered to fill up their bandoliers, and the remaining powder was to be blown up. A three-hour match was set to prevent the explosion warning the Parliamentarians of the Scots' departure but, probably because of the incompetence of the officer concerned, the powder was captured intact.

Their movement screened by the appalling weather, the Scots got away undetected. Yet they made poor progress. "Our march was very sad," wrote one of them, "the way being exceeding deep, the soldiers both wet, hungry and weary."[34] Hamilton was three miles on his way by the time Cromwell discovered that he had gone. Indeed, the Scots escape might have gone undetected longer had it not been for another misfortune so typical of that terrible night. Middleton—probably acting on Hamilton's order sent off at midday on the 17th—brought his cavalry up to rejoin the foot. But there were two main roads between Wigan and Preston, and Middleton chose the easterly one, through Chorley, where he met Langdale, who had been unable to join the Scottish foot after his escape from Preston. Pressing on, Middleton reached the Darwen, only to find his own foot gone and the bridge strongly held. Hamilton had in fact taken the westerly road, through Standish: horse and foot had missed one another by three miles at the most.

Cromwell sent Colonel Francis Thornhagh, with two or three regiments of horse, in pursuit of the Scots, hoping to force them to stand until the rest of his army came up. Thornhagh caught his opponents in Chorley where, "pressing too boldly, [he] was slain, being run into the body and thigh and head by the Enemy's lancers."[35] The Parliamentarian cavalry hung onto the retreating Scots, "killing and taking divers all the way", but Middleton handled the rearguard with considerable skill, and the foot reached Wigan moor, where they drew up. Cromwell followed with 3,000 foot and 2,500 mounted men, leaving Ashton with 4,000 men to hold Preston and its 4,000 prisoners. Fearing that Monro might yet appear and attack Preston, Cromwell authorised Ashton to kill the prisoners if an attack materialised. However, despite Musgrave's urgings, Monro declined to march South.

Hamilton had got away with 7-8,000 foot and 4,000 horse, according to Cromwell's estimate, and, even allowing for the losses on the retreat—Captain Hodgson saw Scots bodies all along the line of march on the 18th—he was still numerically stronger than his pursuers. However, his men were exhausted, demoralised and short of ammunition: the powder in their bandoliers was soaked, and the reserve ammunition had been captured. Hamilton decided to continue the retreat, making for Warrington, where he might buy time by holding or destroying the Mersey bridge, before marching off to join Lord Byron in Wales.

The weary Scots stumbled out of Wigan on the evening of the 18th, having plundered the generally pro-Royalist inhabitants "almost to their skins."[36] Middleton's horse held Cromwell's vanguard just north of the town, and came under heavy pressure as the infantry got away. Turner was marching the last brigade of foot through Wigan when some of Middleton's troopers tore past, and the cry went up that the horse were fleeing and the enemy was at hand. Turner, the professional to his finger-tips, drew up his brigade in the market-place, ready to repulse the attack, but when the cavalry appeared they were a broken regiment of Middleton's. Turner ordered his men to form a lane to allow the fleeing horse to pass through. This manoeuvre might have been easy enough on the drill-ground, but it was another thing in the bright moonlight of another rainy night, with men in the last stages of exhaustion and despair.

But now [wrote Turner] my pikemen, being demented (as I think we all were), would not hear me, and two of them ran full tilt at me. One of their pikes, which was intended for my belly, I gripped with my left hand; the other ran me nearly two inches in the inner side of my right thigh; all of them crying of me and the Horse "They are Cromwell's men. . ." I rode to the Horse and desired them to charge through these Foot. They, fearing the hazard of the pikes, stood. I then made a cry come up from behind them, that the enemy was upon them. This encouraged them to charge my Foot so fiercely that the pikemen threw down their pikes, and got into the houses. All the Horse galloped away, and, as I was aferwards told, rode not through, but over, our whole Foot treading them down.[37]

Cromwell snatched a few hours rest "in the field close by the Enemy; being very dirty and weary, and having marched twelve miles of such grounds as I never rode in all my life, the day being very wet."[38] Several prominent officers and about a hundred other prisoners were taken during the skirmishes of the night, and at first light on the 19th the pursuit went on. Even now there was a flicker of life left in Hamilton's army. In a defile just north of Winwick—"at a place called Redbank", wrote Turner, probably describing a prominent bluff which is still easily visible between Winwick and Newton-le-Willows—the Scots blocked the road with pikemen and lined the hedges with musketeers:

who so rudely entertained the pursuing enemy, that they were compelled to stop until the coming up of Colonel Pride's regiment of foot, who, after a sharp dispute, put those same brave fellows to the run. They were commanded by a little spark in a blue bonnet, who performed the part of an excellent commander, and was killed on the spot.[39]

Cromwell wrote that in this, effectively their last stand, the Scots fought "with great resolution for many hours; ours and theirs coming to push of pike and very close charges..."[40] About 1,000 were killed and 2,000 captured, most of the latter in and around Winwick church.

The action at Winwick not only ended the running battle that had begun three days before: it was the last aggressive act of Hamilton's army. When Cromwell reached Warrington he found that the bridge was strongly fortified, but received word that Baillie sought to negotiate terms of surrender. Hamilton and Callander had departed, leaving Baillie with an order to make what terms he could. On receiving this, Baillie "lost much of that patience of which naturally he was master, and beseeched any that would to shoot him through the head."[41] But he had little alternative but to do as Hamilton had told him. There was no fight left in his men. Cromwell put their number at 4,000, but there may have been fewer, and they were drenched with mud and rain, half-starved and entirely without ammunition. Baillie obtained "quarter for life...and civil usage" for his men, all of whom became prisoners of war.

Hamilton rode towards Chester with the remnants of the cavalry, still hoping to join Byron in North Wales. But he was as undecided in this as in so much else, and, after a dreary night at Malpas in Shropshire, decided to make for Yorkshire. It was an impossible venture. The local trained bands were snapping at their heels, and Lambert was on his way. Lord Traquair and five other Scots peers slipped off to surrender to the Sherrif of Shropshire, and Middleton was captured when his horse fell. These events did little for the morale of Hamilton's men, worn out and mistrustful, and the duke, himself sick, could not pursuade them to leave Uttoxeter on the 24th. There a trumpeter from the Governor of Stafford urged Hamilton to surrender, and there was a brief mutiny when the duke's men, fearing that their senior officers planned to flee, surrounded them within sight of the enemy emissary.

Callander did indeed manage to get away with a few men: he reached London, and escaped to Holland. Langdale, too, made off, but was less fortunate. He reached Nottingham, where he hid in an ale-house with three other officers. "We thought," he admitted, "to have shrouded ourselves as Parliamenteers, and so made no resistance, but were discovered, and are now in Nottingham castle, this 26th of August 1648."[42] Hamilton was discussing terms with the Governor of Stafford when Lambert arrived, and by nightfall on the 25th the duke and his men were prisoners, having "the lives and safety of their persons assured to them."[43]

Preston 1648

"Surely, Sir," declared Cromwell to the Speaker of the House of Commons, "this is nothing but the hand of God."[44] His victory was indeed so impressive that it was hard not to attribute it to divine intervention. Cromwell believed that he had killed 3,000 of the invaders, and captured 10,000, as well as 150 colours. His own losses were light, and seem to have included only three officers of note, Lieutenant-Colonel Cowell, killed at Preston, Colonel Thornhagh, who fell in the pursuit, and Major John Cholmley, killed near Winwick and buried there. However, the Parliamentarian army was almost as exhausted as its opponents: Cromwell described his Horse as "miserably beaten out." The prisoners presented less of a problem than might have been expected. The country people had been so enraged by the Scots' behaviour that they fell upon isolated fugitives, and Cromwell had to issue his own detachments with certificates to ensure that they were not mistaken for Scots and mistreated. Under these circumstances, the disarmed Scots were all too glad of the protection offered by their few guards. "Ten men will keep a thousand from running away," wrote Cromwell.[45]

Having detached Lambert to run Hamilton to earth, Cromwell moved north to deal with Monro as fast as his men's fatigue would permit. It is an indication of the dismal staff-work in Hamilton's army that Monro had heard of Cromwell's arrival at Skipton on 14th August before his commander-in-chief, and, fearing that Cromwell would march against him, Sir George fell back to Appleby. When he discovered that Cromwell had swung West for Preston he marched back to Kirkby Lonsdale, where, just before dawn on the 18th, the first fugitives from Preston spurred into his lines. About 1,200 of Hamilton's rearguard horse made good their escape, and had no intention of remaining in England longer than they could help: Monro begged them to stay with him, but made off to Scotland. Survivors from Langdale's northern horse also came in, and joined the foot regiments of Musgrave and Tyldesley.

Sir Thomas Tyldesley himself, besieging Lancaster Castle, at once rode over and suggested that Monro should collect all the troops in the area—at least 7,000

42

men—and march South to support Hamilton. Munro demurred. He had been ordered to secure himself if Hamilton came under attack, and he was probably a shrewd enough judge of Scottish politics to recognise that his men would be needed at home. He waited two days for further news, and then returned to Scotland by way of Berwick. The Earl of Lanark, Hamilton's vicegerent in Scotland, refused to let the English Royalists cross the border into Scotland, fearing that they would encourage Cromwell, already moving North after Monro, to invade. The Royalists withdrew to Carlisle, and Musgrave and Tyldesley shut themselves up in Appleby Castle. In early October Musgrave received word that Berwick had fallen and Carlisle was about to capitulate. On the 7th, recognising that the castle was not tenable in the face of the heavy guns which would eventually be brought against it, and knowing that the garrison, swollen by fugitives, would soon run out of supplies, he surrendered to Ashton on good terms.[46]

As news of Preston spread, Royalist resistance speedily collapsed in the remainder of England. Colchester surrendered on 28 August; Deal Castle had capitulated a few days before, and Sandown fell shortly afterwards. The rising in North Wales sputtered out, and Lord Byron escaped to the Isle of Man. Pontefract Castle alone held out, and continued its dogged but pointless resistance until March 1649.

The effects of Preston were no less marked in Scotland, where Hamilton's defeat and capture changed the balance of power. Argyll once more became dominant: the Earl of Eglinton raised the Presbyterian West in the "Whiggamore Raid" and marched on Edinburgh, where old Leven secured the castle for the insurgents. The pro-Hamilton Committee of Estates fled to Monro's protection at Stirling. Cromwell, meanwhile, was on the border. He summoned Berwick to surrender, and sent messengers to both the Committee of Estates and Argyll, demanding the restoration of Carlisle and Berwick. On 22 August Cromwell met Argyll at Mordington, on the Scottish side of the Tweed. They agreed that Carlisle and Berwick would be given up, in return for English support against the Engagers in Scotland. Lambert set off for Edinburgh with a strong force of cavalry. Cromwell followed a few days later, and, arriving at the Scottish capital, presented the new

43

Committee of Estates—this time a steadfastly pro-Argyll assembly—with a demand that all who had supported the Engagement should be removed from office in Scotland. Leaving Lambert with two regiments of horse to protect Argyll against any resurgence amongst the Engagers, Crowell set off southwards on 7 October to address himelf to the unanswered question of a constitutional settlement in England.

In his letter to Speaker Lenthall announcing Baillie's capitulation at Warrington, Cromwell did more than point to the part played by God in his victory. He went on to hope that:

you will take courage to do the work of the Lord, in fulfilling the end of your magistracy, in seeking the peace and welfare of the people of this land, that all that will live quietly and peaceably may have countenance from you, and they that are implacable and will not leave troubling the land may speedily be destroyed out of the land.[47]

Parliament showed no sign of fulfilling the army's hopes. The Vote of No Addresses was repealed, and negotiations with the king resumed their tortuous path. The king spun out the talks with his accustomed skill, making concessions he had no intention of honouring, and watching for an opportunity to escape. There was growing dissatisfaction within the army, made more acute when Charles rejected a draft treaty on 16 November, but Fairfax was unwilling to support radical action, and Cromwell, directing operations before Pontefract, was undecided. Matters came to a head when Major-General Henry Ireton prompted the Council of Officers to make direct overtures to the king. On their rejection, the Council presented a Remonstrance to the Commons, demanding that the king should be tried for his life.

When the Commons failed to act, the army moved into action. Charles was taken into its custody and imprisoned in Hurst Castle and on 1 December troops moved into London. The officers announced that they intended to dissolve Parliament, and to constitute a provisional government from its Independent members. The Independents themselves protested at this, and requested that the army should "purge" the existing House. Accordingly, on 6 December, Colonel Pride's regiment of foot, with Colonel Rich's horse in support—both Preston regiments—surrounded the House of Commons. The Presbyterian members—over 240 of them—were excluded, leaving the Independents constituting a Rump of the Commons.

Cromwell arrived in London on the night of Pride's Purge: he had by now decided that there could be no settlement while the king lived. Fairfax disagreed, and, when he recognised the real purpose of the "High Court of Justice", set up by the Rump on 6 January, he would have nothing more to do with it. Charles was duly convicted of "High Treason and other High Crimes", and was beheaded on a scaffold in Whitehall on the afternoon of Tuesday, 30 January 1649.

A new High Court was established in February, to deal with the leaders of the 1648 rebellion and invasion. As a Scottish lord who had surrendered on terms the unfortunate Hamilton might have hoped to escape the full rigour of the court, but he was also Earl of Cambridge in the English peerage, and as such was convicted of high treason. On 9 March he was beheaded outside Westminster Hall, with the English Royalist Lords Holland and Capel. This harshness was not an isolated phenomenon. Two of the Royalist commanders at Colchester, Sir Charles Lucas and Sir George Lisle, had been shot by firing-squad after the city's surrender. Hamilton's Scots were more fortunate. A parliamentary committee was appointed to distinguish between those who had joined Hamilton voluntarily and those who had been pressed into service. The latter were released, giving an undertaking that they would never serve in England again without Parliament's leave. The former, however, were to be dispatched to Virginia or the West Indies as bondsmen: when the colonies had sufficient, the remainder were to be sent to serve under the Venetian Republic.

The search for a constitutional settlement went on, and in December 1653 Cromwell accepted the office of Protector under the Instrument of Government. In May 1657 he declined the Humble Petition and Advice, and with it the kingship, but later the same month accepted a revised Petition, and was installed as Lord Protector under the new constitution. The Protectorate was no more durable than the Protector himself, and after Cromwell's death on 3 September 1658 the nation was once again beset by factionalism and uncertainty ended only with the Restoration of Charles II in 1660.

What of the fortunes of the other principal actors in the drama of August 1648? Callander's estates were confiscated and he himself was imprisoned in 1654, but he was active in politics after the Restoration, and died in 1674. Middleton, captured in Staffordshire, soon escaped—some said that he had broken his parole. He led an abortive rising in Scotland the following year, and took the field with Charles II in 1651, when he was captured at Worcester. He escaped from the Tower, and joined Charles in Holland where he was made an earl in 1656. He did well with the Restoration, becoming commander-in-chief in Scotland and Lord High Commissioner to the Scottish Parliament. Deprived of his office after a bribery scandal in 1663, he later became governor of Tangier, where he died as a result of a fall in 1673. Turner, too, was given military employment by Charles II, commanding the forces in south-west Scotland, where his harshness produced the Pentland Rising of November 1666. Perhaps it is as an author that he is best remembered, and his *Pallas Armata* of 1683 is a useful source for Seventeenth-Century military detail.

It is a cruel irony two of the most attractive of the *dramatis personae* fared worst. Langdale escaped from Nottingham Castle and made his way to Holland, where he was ennobled as Baron Langdale in 1658. But the expense of raising troops in two civil wars, and the confiscations which followed his escape, ruined him: in 1661 he begged to be excused from attending the coronation of Charles II on the grounds that he was too poor. He died the same year. "Honest John" Lambert was Cromwell's second-in-command in Scotland in 1650, and led the decisive attack at Dunbar. He had a horse shot under him at the battle of Worcester the following year. Lambert broke with Cromwell over the question of the Kingship, and the two men were never fully reconciled. He was condemned to death after the Restoration, but a reprieve spared him the ghastly ritual of hanging, drawing and quartering. He died a prisoner, his wits quite gone, in 1683.

John Buchan described Preston as "thus far Oliver's most overwhelming victory," though he added that "it is unnecessary to read undue subtleties into his strategy."[48] The tone of the early stages of the campaign was set as much by Lambert's strategy of indirect defence, threatening the flanks and communications of the invaders, while at the same time covering Yorkshire, as by Hamilton's vacillation and the dissention within the allied high command. Cromwell deserves high praise on several counts. Firstly, despite the bad weather and miry roads, he marched up from Wales with what was lightning speed by the standards of the age. Next, he recognised that his prime duty was to bring about a battle, and he struck hard at Hamilton's centre of gravity. He yet again demonstrated his ability to inspire and encourage as well as to command, and he allowed neither the privation of the approach march nor the euphoria of victory to sever the ties of discipline which bound his army together. Hodgson observed that the public cashiering of Colonel Wren and several of his officers, on a charge of plundering, "gave a great deal of encouragement to the honest part of the army."[49]

It would be wrong to conclude without a word about the thousands of young men who played supporting roles in the drama. The soldiers on both sides endured long marches through rain and mud, without any of the waterproof clothing which has given some comfort to the soldiers of later generations: they carried heavy and cumbersome loads, their bellies empty and their pay in arrears. They fought in weather which would stop a modern football match, on battlefields shrouded in the stinking smoke of black powder, where horrific and painful wounds were common and medical science was in its infancy.

Yet there were moments of sublime courage on both sides: it is hard to stifle admiration for the Royalist musketeers who clung so firmly to the hedges about Ribbleton Moor, the Parliamentarian horse who charged up the miry lane, or the Scots pikemen who died in the defile at Winwick, miles from home, covering the rear of an army which was fast disintegrating. When we consider Preston we should allow neither operational narrative nor historical analysis to obscure the fate of these, the unsung heroes of the drama, who perished doing the duty as they saw it.

1 D. Laing (Ed.) **The Letters and Journals of Mr Robert Baillie,** (3 vols, Edinburgh 1842), III p.51. Baillie (1599-1662) was an influential Presbyterian divine, one of the party sent to wait upon Charles II at the Hague.

2 S. R. Gardiner, "Hamilton, James, 3rd Marquis and 1st Duke of Hamilton..." in **Dictionary of National Biography,** (London 1890), XXIV p.180. Hamilton (1606-49) was educated at Oxford, and succeeded his father as marquis in 1625. He was in favour with Charles I during the 1620s and 30s, although the equivocal part he played in relations between the king and the Covenenters led to his arrest at Oxford in 1643. He had considerable influence in Scotland, particularly amongst the nobility, and was instrumental in persuading the Scottish parliament to vote in favour of military intervention in England in March 1648. Captured after Preston, he was executed on 9 March 1649.

3 Baillie p.45; Sir James Turner, **Memoirs of his own Life and Times** (Edinburgh 1829), p.58. Turner's is a valuable—if not entirely unbiased—account of the campaign and battle, written by an experienced professional soldier. Turner (1615-86?) was educated at Glasgow University, but followed a military career from 1632 onwards, serving in the Swedish, Scottish and king's armies. Sir Walter Scott modelled his character Dugald Dalgetty in part on Turner.

4 Quoted in "Turner, Sir James" in **Dictionary of National Biography** LVII p.340.

5 Baillie I pp.43-44.

6 Captain Samuel Birch, "A true and perfect account...", in **Historical Manuscripts Commission, 14th Report, Appendix part II, MSS of His Grace the Duke of Portland,** Vol III, (London 1894), p.174. Birch was an infantry company commander in Ashton's Lancashire brigade, and played a prominent part in the battle for Walton Bridge.

7 Turner p.59.

8 Birch p.173. For the organization of armies of the period see C. H. Firth's old but magisterial **Cromwell's Army** (London 1902, and many later editions) and Peter Young and Wilfred Emberton **The Cavalier Army** (London 1974). Philip Haythornthwaite's **The English Civil War: An Illustrated Military History,** is a most readable popular work capably researched by an enthusiast. It is particularly helpful on matters of dress and equipment. For the Civil War in Lancashire, see J. J. Bagley and A. S. Lewis, **Lancashire at War,** (Dalesman Publishing Co. 1977).

9 "Sir Philip Musgrave's Relation" in **Miscellany of the Scottish History Society** (Edinburgh 1904) II p.302.

10 Gilbert Burnet, **The Memoirs of the Lives and Actions of James and William Dukes of Hamilton and Castle-Harold,** (Oxford 1852), p.450. Bishop Burnet wrote this in 1673. Although he was not personally present at the battle, he had access to well-placed Scottish sources, and seems to have read Turner's account.

11 Newssheet of 21 August 1648 quoted in G. Ormerod (Ed), **Tracts relating to Military Proceedings in Lancashire. . .** (Chetham Society 1844), p.254.

12 Quoted in S. R. Gardiner (Ed), **The Hamilton Papers,** (Camden Society 1880), p.213.

13 Birch pp.174-5.

14 Burnet p.453.

15 Ibid. and S. R. Gardiner, **History of the Great Civil War, 1642-1649,** (4 vols, London 1898), IV p.181.

16 Contemporary newssheet **The Moderate,** Thomason Tracts E.457.21. George Thomason, a London bookseller, collected a large amount of contemporary newssheets and tracts in the period 1640-1661. **The Moderate Intelligencer** for 17-24 August 1648 (E.460.35) is useful for the battle, and other tracts (notably **A Letter from Holland,** E.467.21) throw intermittent light on the campaign. J. Rushworth's **Historical Collections** (London 1659-1701) are also of occasional use.

17 Original Memoirs written during the Civil War. . .Memoirs of Captain Hodgson (Edinburgh 1806). p.114. Hodgson's memoirs are unreliable for both spelling and dates, but they give an unrivalled description of the battle against Langdale south of Ribbelton Lane.

18 For accounts of this important meeting see Turner p.62, Burnet p.450, and Sir Marmaduke Langdale, "An Impartial relation of the late Fight at Preston. . ." in Ormerod **Tracts** p.267. Langdale wrote this (which is understandably not impartial) while in prison at Nottingham immediately after the campaign. Clarendon's account of Preston, in **The History of the Rebellion** (8 vols, London 1826), VI pp.71-76, relies heavily upon Langdale's version and upon conversations between Langdale and Clarendon. The anonymous author of **A Letter from Holland** (E.467.21), a Royalist who had failed to gain employment in Hamilton's army because he had previously opposed the Covenant, suggests that the discussion took place at Kirkby Thore. It seems likely that on 13 August the council at Hornby discussed the question which had already been debated at Kirkby Thore in late July.

19 Cromwell to William Lenthall, Speaker of the House of Commons, 20 August 1648, quoted in Thomas Carlyle (Ed), **Oliver Cromwell's Letters and Speeches. . .** (3 vols, London 1846), I p.370. Cromwell wrote four important letters during the campaign. On 17 August he penned a hasty note to the Lancashire

Committee, telling it of his victory at Preston and asking it to "raise your county; and to improve your forces" to ensure the total ruin of the Scots. His letter to Speaker Lenthall, written from Warrington on 20 August, gives a more complete account of the battle. On the same day Cromwell warned the Yorkshire Committee to be on the lookout for Scottish stragglers, and he gave the same committee more details from Wigan on the 23rd. All are printed in Carlyle and in the more complete W. C. Abbot (Ed), **The Writings and Speeches of Oliver Cromwell,** (4 vols, Cambridge 1937) I.

20 Ibid. p.371.

21 Langdale p.267.

22 Turner p.62.

23 Hodgson p.115, Carlyle I p.371.

24 Quoted in W. Beamont (Ed) **A Discourse of the War in Lancashire,** (Chetham Society 1864), p.65.

25 Carlyle I p.371, Hodgson p.115. The topography of the battlefield can be reconstructed with some certainty from maps in the County Record Office. A strip-map (DDX 194/28), probably compiled for Dr Richard Kuerden in the 1680s, shows the line of Ribbleton Lane and indicates some buildings and enclosures, and DX/838, an Eighteenth Century Ribbleton Hall Estate map, shows Ribbleton Moor and some of the enclosures. The 1849 Ordnance Survey is also useful. My own map of Preston and its surroundings is based upon these, and the considerable additional research of Mr Alistair Hodge.

26 Hodgson p.116.

27 Carlyle I p.372.

28 Ibid p.373.

29 Hodgson pp.118-9.

30 Langdale p.268. Langdale repeated this complaint to Clarendon. "And Sir Marmaduke Langdale told me often afterwards," wrote Clarendon, "that he verily believed, if one thousand foot had been sent to him he should have gained the day." (Clarendon VI p.74). Langdale also bitterly resented the fact that the Scots had not secured Watery Lane.

31 Burnet p.455.

32 Birch p.175.

33 Turner p.63, Burnet p.455.

34 Burnet p.457.

35 Carlyle I p.374.

36 Ibid. p.375.

37 Turner pp.66-7.

38 Carlyle I p.375.

39 Quoted in Carlyle I pp.368-9.

40 Ibid. p.373. Hodgson admitted that the Scots foot were drawn up "in a most advantageous place, and snaffled our forlorn [advanced guard], and put them to retreat" (p.122). The action at Winwick deserves more emphasis than it generally receives, and indicates that the Scots were still capable of fighting hard despite the miseries of the past few days. It is yet more evidence that Hamilton would haver fared far better had he determined to offer battle on Walton Hill on the 18th, using his robust foot to best advantage.

41 Burnet p.458.

42 Langdale p.269.

43 Burnet p.458.

44 Carlyle I p.378.

45 Carlyle I p.379.

46 Musgrave p.303; see also the newssheet "A Great Victory at Appleby", in Ormerod **Tracts.**

47 Carlyle I p.378.

48 John Buchan, **Oliver Cromwell** (London 1944) p.283.

49 Hodgson p.123.